SENTNESS INTERACTIVE

DEVELOPING THE APOSTOLIC WITHIN YOU

SENTNESS INTERACTIVE

DEVELOPING THE APOSTOLIC WITHIN YOU

Bob and Mary Bain

Open Wells Publishing

Shilbottle, Northumberland, United Kingdom
Bob and Mary Bain
e-mail: bobbain@hotmail.co.uk

CONTENTS

PART FOUR – DEEPER WITH JESUS

POEMS

LIST OF IMAGES

The full list of images with acknowledgements is on page 198.
Colour versions of these pictures can be found in the Resources
section of **welcomenetwork.org**

In appreciation of:-

All those who have been sent with us on this journey with Jesus.

We especially want to say thank you to Paul and Cilla Hollamby and others for testing out some of the materials and giving feedback, and to Jenny Reid for her enthusiasm for the project, and her daughter, Anna, for her inspirational cover design ideas.

INTRODUCTION

This short handbook encourages us to develop the apostolic within us, as a vital part of our growing-up process.

God wants to develop and mature us, so we can enjoy His abundant life more and more, as we journey through life. There is great joy in knowing who we are, where we are going, and having a sense of God's calling and purpose for us. Being apostolic is really about staying true to that calling, allowing God to shape and establish us step by step.

God gives us a whole bunch of people to help us on our way. Look out for them! God has put them in your life with your good in mind, to be a blessing and benefit to you.

In turn, may you become yourself, more and more a blessing and benefit to those around you!

Jesus said,
'I have come that they may have life, and have it to the full'
John 10:10

HOW TO USE THIS HANDBOOK

This is an interactive workbook – please write in it!
Spend some time thinking about the questions asked and try to answer them in your own words, filling in the blanks as you do so.

You may want to work through the different sessions in a daily time with God, or perhaps weekly, with another person, or a small group, so that you, and others, can benefit from some sharing conversations.

Be alert and prayerful about what God may be especially saying to you.

You will probably need a bit of time to reflect on each section as you go through the book. We have added a review point at the end of each of the four sections. We suggest that you don't rush on ahead, but spend a short time looking back and noting down things you want to remember.

Let the pictures, poems and scriptures speak to you. Reflect upon them inside your head, and let God personally unpack each one. You will find that He has some wonderful surprises for you as you do this. There is always more to discover!

PART ONE
PURPOSE &
DIRECTION

God wants to wake us up to
our purpose and direction in life.

INTERACTIVE ONE - 'SENTNESS'

God wants to wake us up to our purpose and direction in life.
He gives us that sense of being SENT.

As a child, the house where we lived was surrounded by commercial glasshouses, full of tomatoes and cucumbers, and in my late teens, it was easy to get vacation jobs picking the cucumbers, because my father knew one of the owners. My motive was money, and I wasn't really interested in working hard for it, or even doing a good job! In my first year after becoming a Christian, my attitude didn't improve. I was too full of myself and what I thought about the working conditions and how appalling the pay was. Therefore I worked begrudgingly, and was a complete timewaster. I used to take toilet breaks between the breaks! I'm sure I would have lost the job, but for the fact that it was just for a few weeks and the foreman was aware my dad knew the owner.

By the next summer though, something amazing had happened. I had taken to heart a wonderful bible verse - Colossians 3:23 – *'Whatever your task, work at it with all your heart as serving the Lord not men'*. I was determined to do better at my summer vacation job. What a pleasant surprise the foreman had during my first week back! On the first day, when I showed up, you should have seen how his face dropped! I could almost hear the words on his lips, 'Oh no, not him again!' However, I got on with the job, going up and down the tall rows of cucumber plants in the glasshouse with a hand cart, steadily filling it up with cucumbers. The conditions were humid and dirty, but I kept my joy and worked hard, with a good heart. The foreman was amazed, and I really felt God had given me an opportunity to show Him off in a better light than I had done the previous year.

I had been bad news to the foreman, but now I was showing, by my changed attitude and hard work, that I was different. In Bible terms, I was becoming more like 'the aroma of Christ', God wanted me to be. Others also noticed the change, and wanted to know what had happened to me.

Whatever God's purpose and direction for our lives, wherever He sends us, you can be sure He wants our whole hearts engaged in it. In this way, we become His beautiful scent in the process.

A BOTTLE OF SCENT

What might the Holy Spirit be saying to you through this picture, about who you are and your purpose in life?
Write down one or two thoughts below.

_____

_____

_____

_____

_____

_____

_____

_____

_____

_____

*"Our lives are a Christ-like **SCENT, an aroma, a perfume** rising up to God…and noticed by others"* 2 Corinthians 2:15

This Bible verse tells us that there is a God-given, spiritual scent about believers, that can influence and bring life and blessing to others. Let us understand what happened to us when we received Jesus into our lives. It's not a case of us having a bottle of spiritual scent with us, from which we occasionally dab ourselves, rather this verse tells us that **our whole lives _are_ the scent** – who we are, what we do, how we act and how we behave.

We are called to be a fragrant aroma that God wants to release on an unsuspecting world, even as we walk into the room. People are used to bad attitudes. They don't expect people to be loving and caring, certainly not beyond the superficial. The scent of God in us is a wake-up call to those around us.

This is God's plan, to wake people up to a new life in Him. We are to spread the beautiful fragrance of Jesus Christ, wherever we are sent in life. We are His scent, being sent – called to be a blessing to those around us. You may not feel much of a blessing, but God does not have a plan B - you really do have within you all that is needed. Paul writes in Philippians 1:6, for example, that the good work started within us, when we said 'Yes' to Jesus, will be completed. Peter tells us that we were born to be a blessing on this earth (1Peter 3:9). What God begins in us, He is able to finish.

Funnily enough, the scent we bring into a room not only brings blessing to others, but also wakes them up to their own calling. We almost cannot help it; our fragrance brings out from others the response of a yes or a no, to their own call from God. Christ's scent of 'sentness' in us brings a reaction of either acceptance or rejection from others, as they wake up to His call to them.

As Paul puts it in 2 Corinthians 2:15, we are a fragrance to others that leads to life, or a smell that leads to death.

Being God's 'scent on legs' is foundational to our understanding of what it means to be apostolic.

The word, 'apostle' literally means a 'sent one' – *someone sent by someone else, on a journey with a purpose; carrying the authority of the one who sent them, to represent that person, just as if he, himself was present.*

So, each of us is sent by Jesus to represent Him to others. We may not all be apostles, but we should all smell apostolic, because we have all been sent!

To be apostolic is to have a scent of 'sentness' about us; to understand that we have a calling and a purpose for our lives from Jesus, to be a blessing to this world.

PRAYER

Lord, please help us to develop the apostolic within us, so that we can introduce You to others, and help them to wake up to Your purpose and direction for their lives. Amen.

AN ARROW BEING RELEASED

One of our sons really loves archery, and it's probably all our fault! When he was young, we went on a family trip to Sherwood Forest, famous as the home of Robin Hood, and while we were there, we bought him a bow and some arrows, with rubber bungs on the end of them. He dressed up as a mini-Robin Hood and had a great time! The rest is history; along with a professional adult bow, he now also has several swords, and from time to time has been involved in the re-enactment of medieval battles. What an influence we can have as parents! My son's bow is enormous, and would be unusable in my hands, but in his, the arrows released are deadly, unswervingly hitting the target!

In the Bible, there is an unusual description given for sons as 'arrows in the hand of a warrior. Why do you think this surprising description might be a good one? If you are in a group, share what you think with one another.
The actual words used are these - *'Like arrows in the hand of a warrior are sons born in one's youth'* Psalm 127:4

_____

_____

_____

_____

_____

When we accept Jesus as our Lord and Saviour, we become sons of God.
What might it mean for you, as His child, to be an arrow in the hand of our Father God?

_____

_____

_____

_____

_____

_____

_____

_____

_____

We have all experienced moments when something is just about to begin. What do you think God might be saying to you through the picture of an arrow about to be released?

_____

_____

_____

_____

_____

_____

_____

_____

_____

_____

_____

_____

As children of God, we are being released into His plans and purposes for our lives. God wants us to be sharp arrows in His hands, set in the direction that He has for us. If we are willing, God is ready to release us, to get us to the place where we are meant to go. In this way, as His sons, we can represent Him in the place where we land.

A WORD OF RELEASE

In our early thirties, with a family of two young boys, both Mary and I felt that God wanted us to be stretched by doing some kind of specific ministry training. We really weren't sure what that might look like! At first, I thought that God might be telling us to go on a short-term mission experience, with a particular organization that has bases all over the world. It was an appealing and exciting prospect, but in the end, I realized that its appeal for me was really about travelling overseas, rather than for any great spiritual reason.

In the end, we opted for something much more ordinary looking, and even a bit academic, but it was a specific word from the Lord that got us there! He knew the appeal that alliteration has for me so, as we were weighing up whether to travel overseas, or to go to a bible college called Mattersey, this alliterative phrase popped into my mind, that 'what mattered, was Mattersey!' It felt like God had given us a definite word of release! Others may have felt that this was a bit daft, but it enabled us to fill in the application forms for the Bible college with the confidence that God was in it. It might not have given *you* confidence, but God knew just what would hit the spot for me. He knows each one of us through and through, and what are the words, or set of circumstances, which will uniquely speak to us, and guide us in the right direction.

Can you think of any specific situations, or words from God, that have been important to you?
What was their impact on you?

Were you released into something new through them? Think of a couple of examples to write down below.
If you are in a group, share with one another your examples.

Example 1.

_____

_____

_____

_____

_____

_____

_____

_____

_____

_____

Example 2.

_____

_____

_____

_____

_____

_____

_____

_____

_____

_____

_____

_____

_____

_____

_____

_____

STUCK!

Years ago, when I was in my twenties, I innocently got into a car with my brother-in-law. We were parked in a cul-de-sac of terraced houses, with a brick wall facing us at the far end. Suddenly, he drove straight at the brick wall at a very fast speed, and then put the handbrake on at the last possible second! In a flash, we were facing the opposite direction! To put it mildly, I was shocked silly and then very relieved! He had been showing off his advanced driving skills, but some changes in direction could do with being a little less dramatic!

However, this incident does makes me think about the truth that there are no dead ends in our journey with God. All I could see was a brick wall, but there was a way forward, however spectacular! If we are feeling stuck in a dead end, it is not the end of our story - God can change our direction and bring us through.

Do we feel as if nothing is happening right now in our lives? Are there some specific things that God has spoken about, that we sense need to be released at this time? Are we ready for His way forward, however spectacular that might be?

_____

_____

_____

_____

_____

_____

_____

_____

_____

_____

_____

_____

_____

PRAYER

Lord, we are ready to be released in whatever direction You have next for us.

We are up for any change in our situation that is needed.

Please, Lord, give us the wisdom and knowledge we need for each day. May we also be open for this wisdom to come through others.

You may have spoken to us in the past and we've forgotten, or haven't understood the relevance of Your words for this moment we are in. Please remind us, so we can understand better the bigger picture of what is going on in our lives. Amen.

INTERACTIVE TWO -
POSITIONED BY THE SPIRIT

'The wind blows wherever it pleases. You hear its sound, but you cannot tell where it comes from or where it is going. So it is with everyone born of the Spirit'. John 3:8

Dandelions are a very common flower in our part of the world, and, after they have flowered ,they produce Dandelion clocks - circles of seeds, all ready to be scattered by the wind. As a child, I would help in the scattering process. Blowing dandelion clocks was part and parcel of my childhood. I loved watching the seeds float off as I blew; they would catch the breeze and go wherever it carried them.

The Bible describes the Holy Spirit like a wind that blows wherever He pleases, and so it is with each one of us. We are blown by Him, like dandelion seeds, and carried wherever He determines. He can blow us anywhere, and we might think it all a bit random, and not understand why we have landed where we have landed. In reality, God positions us very specifically in particular places, however random it may have felt. As we are blown, our hopes and dreams go with us; and they are released in just the right place, at just the right time. He sets us up as He chooses, and who can argue with that, because after all He is God? Wherever we are, we have been positioned by the Spirit. We must be ready – He may choose to move us again. Whatever His plans for us, we can be sure they are intended for our good.

MOVIE MOMENT!

There is an old British movie I can totally recommend to you called, **'I know where I'm going'** (you can find it on youtube). The heroine thinks she has her life all worked out - what she is going to do and who she is going to marry, but she is in for some surprises...

You may want to get some popcorn and sit down for a movie moment with us, and see what happened.

Well what did you think? Sorry it was in black and white, but we hope you enjoyed it and got the point! What do you think the main message of the movie was?

_____

_____

_____

_____

_____

_____

_____

_____

_____

_____

_____

_____

Like the dandelion seeds, we don't *really* know where we are going when we set off, but later we may begin to appreciate that the Holy Spirit has been at work, and every unexpected twist and turn in the direction of our lives has been necessary. Even the stormier moments we experienced were there for a reason.

JACOB WAKES UP

Read Genesis 28:10-22

In this passage, Jacob wakes up from an amazing dream – he sees a vision of a ladder from God to the earth on which angels are descending and ascending. At this time, he is in the middle of a perfect storm. He is on the run from his outraged brother, Esau, and heading towards his greedy uncle, Laban. This is what he thinks he is doing, but his thinking is too limited. Actually, God has much more in mind. In the middle of all this stormy weather, God gives him a dream that changes his understanding of what is really going on. There is a bigger picture for him to consider.

After his dream of the ladder, what does Jacob wake up and say (Gen. 28:16)?

_____

_____

_____

_____

Jacob called the place Bethel, which means House of God. What else could he have named it! He recognised that during the night, he had had an amazing encounter with God. Just when he thought he was all alone and abandoned, God was preparing him for the next phase in his life, and reassuring him that he was not alone. He wasn't fleeing to Laban at all, God was with him, and was sending him there.

The experiences of the next few years would change Jacob, and he would return home a different person. All sorts of things would happen through God sending him to his uncle. For example, despite his own evil plans to prevent it, Laban would witness how much Jacob had prospered, and that this was the favour of God at work in Jacob's life. Furthermore, Jacob would learn to walk by faith, trusting that God would help him. As a result, he would become economically established and start a family. Jacob's life had been in God's hands all the way through - God's good plans had been worked out!

'All the days ordained for me in your book were written before any of them came to be.' Psalm 139:16

God wants to wake us up to His plans and purpose for our lives.
Why do you think God has got you where you are at this stage of your life?
Sit down for a moment and reflect.

_____

_____

_____

_____

_____

_____

_____

_____

_____

_____

_____

_____

Have there been some <u>pleasant surprises</u> along the way, as God has positioned you where you are today? *(e.g. with family, health changes, work opportunities, money, relationships, moving points)*
Write down some of them.

_____

_____

_____

_____

_____

_____

_____

_____

_____

_____

_____

_____

_____

BEING OPEN

We need to open our eyes to see the steps that God has for our lives. He also has things to say to us, so we need to listen up with open ears.

As an example for us, what does Jesus say that He does in John 5:19 ?

_____

_____

_____

_____

_____

Who will help us with what we are to say, and how we are to say it?
Luke 12:11-12 (cf. Matthew 10:19-20)

_____

_____

_____

_____

_____

What decision was made after a group of believers began to seek God in Acts 13:1-3 ?

_____

_____

_____

_____

Good decisions are best made through seeking God's wisdom and counsel. In Acts chapter 13, the first missionary journey of Paul and Barnabas is described – a major turning point in the spreading of the gospel message across the world. When we worship and pray, spending time with God, He can lead us on, into important, fresh directions. Our own effectiveness in life is dependent on our relationship with God, so we need to be open to see, and to hear what He might be saying to us, through His Holy Spirit.

PRAYER

Father, I want to be open to listen and to understand Your specific plans and direction for my life, at this time.

I am willing to <u>learn</u> from You, to <u>listen</u> and <u>follow</u> Your guidance.

Holy Spirit, please help me to be ready to step out in what You show me to do.

Thank you that You promise to be with me wherever I go.

Amen.

INTERACTIVE THREE - OPENING DOORS

What is the primary reason we are located in the place where we are? We might think we are living there for educational or work reasons, because we want to be near the grandchildren, or because we were born there. In whatever is going on, we can be sure that God has opened the door and positioned us, so that we can fulfil His purposes and plans.

What does Acts 17:26 have to say about this thought?

_____

_____

_____

God opens doors to the specific places He has for us, and shuts the doors on others. To the church at Philadelphia, Jesus calls Himself the one *'who holds the key of David. What he opens no-one can shut, and what he shuts no-one can open...I have placed before you an open door that no-one can shut...'* (Rev.3:7-8). This is very reassuring! If a door needs opening for us to walk through, we can trust that God will open it, and also that He will make it clear when we are to walk through it.

Paul the apostle thought in terms of doors needing to be opened or shut.
What does Paul ask the Colossians to do for him in Colossians 4:3?

_____

_____

_____

Why was Paul staying on in Ephesus? (1 Cor 16:9)

_____

_____

_____

_____

_____

_____

Jesus is the One to whom we need to cry out, so that we can step out effectively into the things God wants for us.

Here is a lovely prayer promise, where Jesus says something so famous that, in our familiarity with the words, we may need to pause or it may just wash over us.

'Ask and it will be given to you; seek and you will find; knock and the door will be opened to you' (Mt.7:7).

Pray that the Lord will open the doors that need opening and will shut the doors that need shutting. Ask Him how you can step out into the things He wants for your life, in the different places where He has positioned you.
If you are in a group, you can pray in pairs for one another about this.

God wants us to be good stewards wherever He has placed us, and to be diligent in all the daily details presented to us. He will give us the keys to help us, so that the right doors can be opened and shut. God, also, wants to give us the wisdom to understand His perfect timing in everything we do.

INTERACTIVE FOUR - STICK WITH JESUS

'If you abide in me and I abide in you, you will bear much fruit. Apart from me you can do nothing' John 15:5

This section is all about our hearts. There is an old Christmas cracker joke, that Mary and I really love, 'What did the stamp say to the envelope? Stick with me, baby and together we will go places!' Jesus wants us to stick with Him. When He arrives in our lives, we start to go places. When we hear Him knock, let's welcome Him in. Apart from Him we can do nothing.

'Behold I stand at the door and knock. If anyone hears my voice and opens the door, I will come in and eat with him and he with me'. Rev. 3:20

Eating together is a very friendly way to describe how Jesus wants to relate with us. As we spend time with Him, He helps us to understand that things can be done differently now. Good changes start as we open the door, and let His way of doing things into our lives.

Read through the poem below, which was written just before a major change Bob and I made, when we moved from one part of the country to another.

Pick out one line which you particularly sense that God is highlighting to you.

Surrender

You are showing me the way of surrender
I can lay down my burdens,
Everything falling at Your feet.
Only You
It is only You I long for,
Only You.
I give myself, my needs, my failings;

"Keep bowing your head, dear one,
There is joy in taking the yoke
Beside Me."

When I lower my head
And agree that Your will,
Not mine, be done
I find my soul is washed over,
Flooded with peace.
There is no need to worry
No reason to fear
Because I am held, kept safe
With You.

I feel the warmth of Your love
Within, and all around me,
Sometimes so intense...
And I know it is Your love
Burning inside me.
I ask You to break my heart
So that my heart is like Yours.
Open, vulnerable, compassionate and feeling
Not distant, remote, detached and cold,
Like my heart more naturally would be!

If my heart is broken,
The warmth of Your love,
The light of Your goodness,
The image of Your being
Can shine forth;
As I surrender-
Giving myself to You, in love,
Bowing my head under Your yoke,
Your glory flows out from my life.

O, the wonder of being part of Your plan!
Together, holding out the invitation-
"Come, come to Jesus,
Come meet Your loving Father,
Come be filled to overflowing with His gentle Holy Spirit!"
Jesus, here I am,
Your love slave;
I am setting out with you, today
Please hold my hand.
How can I fear when we are yoked together?

Mary Bain   March 2017   (Mt.11:28-30)

What line did you pick out? Why did you choose that one?

_____

_____

_____

_____

_____

_____

_____

_____

_____

_____

_____

Now read through the poem again with this question in mind:-
Are there attitudes or behaviors in your heart that God is highlighting, and asking you to surrender to Him?

_____

_____

_____

_____

_____

_____

_____

_____

_____

_____

_____

_____

_____

_____

_____

'Come to me all you who are weary and heavy-laden, and I will give you rest. Take my yoke upon you and learn of me, for I am meek and lowly in heart and you shall find rest for your souls. For my yoke is easy and my burden is light'. Matthew 11:28-30

Jesus tests our heart to see whether we are willing to
- come to Him,
- take His yoke upon us and
- learn from Him.

A few years ago, I discovered something which I found really encouraging, when I was looking at this verse. In Jesus' time, when the farmer put his oxen under the yoke, there were always two oxen, usually a younger ox with an older one, so that the younger could learn from the older. I realized that in these verses, when Jesus invites us to take His yoke upon us, He is actually saying, 'Come under My yoke, I am walking right next to you, you can learn from Me.'

That's why His yoke is easy, because Jesus is there under it with us. We are learning on the job with Him, and relying on His strength, as He takes the strain alongside us!

PRAYER

Lord Jesus,

Thank you that you understand how we can feel tired and weary, and how we often try to live our lives and serve others in our own strength.

Today we are saying, 'Yes, we are willing to come to You again; we are willing to step into Your yoke and learn from You. We are willing to surrender our own ideas and make You the centre of our lives. Amen

INTERACTIVE FIVE - STEPPING OUT

We can step out without fear and anxiety because God has chosen the way for us.

'The Lord will instruct them in the way they should go.'
(Psalm 25:12)

Moses is a good example of a man who was sent by God. In Exodus chapters three and four, we see how Moses had to be woken up to who he was, and to realize that God was sending him on a mission.

Skim read through Exodus chapter three, and spot all the places where the word 'sent' or 'go' are used. How many did you find? *(see page 201 for our count)*

_____

Did you notice how reluctant Moses was to change direction, and how many reasons he had why he couldn't do what God wanted him to do? In a similar way, we can have our excuses and be reluctant to step out in the calling which we believe God has given us (we are, after all, just human!).

Spot the THREE excuses Moses makes to God.
What does Moses say to God, and what is the gist of how God replies in ... ?

Exodus 4:1 ?

Moses says

_____

_____

_____

_____

God replies

_____

_____

_____

_____

_____

Exodus 4:10 – 12 ?

Moses says

_____

_____

_____

_____

God replies

_____

_____

_____

_____

_____

Exodus 4:13 ?

Moses says

_____

_____

_____

_____

God replies

_____

_____

_____

_____

What things might stop you, or make you reluctant to step out in God's calling, now or in the past?

If you are with others, you may be able to share together in small groups, after some individual reflection time.

_____

_____

_____

_____

_____

_____

_____

_____

_____

_____

_____

_____

All the time that Moses was making excuses, God knew he was the right person for the job. Eventually, Moses gave up objecting, because the Lord kept giving him reassuring answers, and finally he set off on what turned out to be the adventure of a lifetime.

This is what the Lord is opening up for each one of us – the adventure of a lifetime. We may not be feeling especially adventurous, and we may have a whole stack of good reasons why the Lord might just possibly have got it wrong. But, of course, we really do know God has not got it wrong, and He knows what is best for our lives. Just as with Moses, God has an answer to every objection, excuse, fear and anxiety that we can come up with. In fact, He is the answer!

REASSURING WORDS
God loves to give personal, reassuring words to help us, so that we don't get anxious or fearful.

Here is one Bible passage full of reassuring words to reflect on.

'I took you from the ends of the earth, from its furthest corners I called you. I said, "You are my servant". I have chosen you and have not rejected you.
So do not fear, for I am with you. Do not be dismayed for I am your God. I will strengthen you and help you; I will uphold you with my righteous right hand.'(Isa 41:9-10).

It may be helpful for you to take in these words and make them your own.
Read the passage through slowly, pausing every so often, then read it again several times more.
As you read, listen to the words and imagine God is speaking to you, straight into your heart.

Receive the strength and love that God wants to pour into you through His words.

When you finish, pray the words back to Him with thankfulness.

You may want to write something down as a prayerful response to Him..

_____

_____

_____

_____

_____

_____

_____

_____

_____

_____

Jesus describes His words as a solid rock on which we can build our lives (Matthew 7:24-27)

What is promised in the Bible in ...?

Proverbs 3:5-6?

_____

_____

_____

_____

_____

Philippians 4:19?

_____

_____

_____

_____

_____

Not all callings are as dramatic as that of Moses. Some of us may just have a growing awareness of who we are, and what God has called us to do. Sometimes, God speaks words to us over a period of time, that later come together and begin to make sense.

Share an example of an encounter with God, which involved stepping out into something new, either from your own personal experience, or someone you know.

_____

_____

_____

_____

_____

_____

_____

_____

_____

_____

_____

_____

_____

PRAYER

Thank you, Father God, that there is a unique calling on my life. You have shown me that there are things you want me to do, and no-one else.

Help me to embrace the adventure of my calling! I know that you have chosen me and promise to be with me, even giving me the right words to speak.

I want to step out, trusting always in Your provision and guidance.

Help me not to be fearful, thinking I am not good enough.

I choose to receive the strength You provide, as I daily walk, by Your side, on the path You have chosen for me.

Amen.

INTERACTIVE SIX -
ALL NEEDED

The eye cannot say to the hand, 'I don't need you!' And the head cannot say to the feet, 'I don't need you!'
(1 Cor.12:21)

We are all needed in the body of Christ.

We are on an important mission; sent to bring the presence of Jesus into people's lives. No-one else can be you! Your piece in the jigsaw is needed.

God has sent us <u>all</u> out into His harvest field, and calls us His fellow workers. We are considered by God to be His friends and partners in the work of bringing mankind back to Him (2 Cor.6:1). God addresses our low self-esteem, and the lies that tell us we are useless and unnecessary to His plans. He tells us rather that we are all loved and needed (see also 1 Cor.12:20-21).

Let's apply these words of Paul to ourselves, and be at peace, *'By the grace of God I am what I am, and his grace to me was not without effect...'* (1 Cor.15:10). God's grace is enough for us – we are who we are. Paul felt unworthy to be called an apostle (1 Cor.15:9) because of his past, yet he accepted and received God's grace to become who God had called him to be.

<u>Write down</u> what you think the Holy Spirit would want you to draw in the jigsaw piece outline overleaf.
Try to express something about <u>who you are in the body of Christ</u> from God's point of view *(your heart, your gifts, your abilities, your personality and the experiences which have shaped your life)*

_____

_____

_____

_____

_____

_____

_____

_____

_____

_____

_____

_____

_____

_____

Try to draw what you have written about in the jigsaw outline, If you like, get some crayons and colour it in.

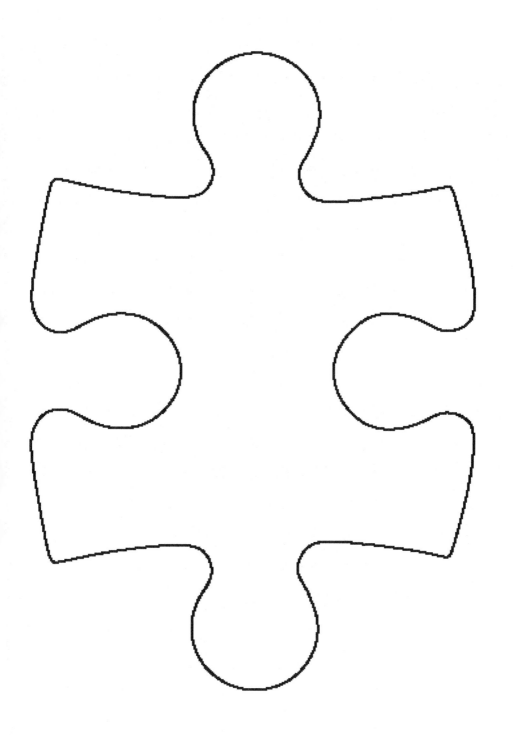

The Missing Piece

God needs me to serve Him
If I do not do it, no one else will.
There will be a gap!
There is a place in His heart, His plan,
That has my shape in it.
I am chosen to do my part
To be who He has called me to be.
I am part of the jigsaw,
And so are you.
Not just believers,
But those who are not yet believers too!
There is a place for all of us;
That is why we must find others,
Tell them to "Come and see;
While there is still time
To complete the jigsaw."

We are all needed!
Find your place,
His heart is aching for you. Yes, you!
You are the piece He is missing!
Being that piece,
Coming to Him and laying down,
You will find the peace
That you have been missing.
You will know, that all along
You have always been in His heart;
So special to Him!
Chosen to be with Him,
Chosen to be loved,
Chosen to serve.

Mary Bain April 2021

Pick a line or a phrase in the poem which leaps out at you.
Why did you choose that line or phrase?

_____

_____

_____

_____

_____

_____

_____

_____

_____

_____

_____

_____

_____

_____

TWO DONKEYS

Let's look at a story in Matthew's gospel about two donkeys who were needed by Jesus.

Read Matthew 21:1-11

Two disciples are sent to get two donkeys, a mother and her colt. Jesus tells the disciples exactly where to find them, that they are to untie them and bring them back to him. These two donkeys were going to be involved with Jesus at an important moment in His mission. How amazing that a a young colt, which had never been ridden before was about to carry Jesus into the centre of Jerusalem!

What a wonderful picture of how we, too, are released into our own mission with Jesus. Applying this story to ourselves, we can see that just like the donkeys, Jesus really does know how to find us, wherever we may be and whatever our situation. We may have got ourselves into a complete mess, or be tied up and in the wrong place, but He can get us back on track! He knows where to find us. However there can be challenges along the way. There may be people who, for various reasons, would rather we didn't go along with God's plans for our lives.

When the disciples were untying the donkeys, who challenged them in these verses?

Mark 11:5-6?

_____

_____

_____

Luke 19:33?

_____

_____

_____

'What are you doing, untying that colt?' (Mt.21:3).

What answer were the disciples told to give when challenged about the donkeys?

_____

_____

_____

When we are released to be of service to the Lord, we may similarly encounter opposition to God's plan and purpose. Let's have the courage to step out with Jesus, saying the words he told his disciples to say if challenged, 'The Lord needs me to do this'.

The Body of Jesus is made up of many parts; each part must do its work (Eph.4:16), and every part is needed. We all have our different and unique roles to play.

Why do you think the mother donkey may have been needed?

_____

_____

_____

_____

_____

When Jesus arrives at the Temple in the centre of Jerusalem, He clears out the 'den of robbers' and calls it a House of Prayer for all nations. Both donkeys had a significant part to play on this important day in Jesus' life. If you had asked them, at the start of their day, they wouldn't have guessed what was about to happen to them!

PRAYER

Dear Lord Jesus, please help me to accept my place in Your Body. I know that I am needed just as much as any other person.

Help me to grow in confidence in my calling, both in who I am and in what I do. May I not compare myself with other people, but have the courage to be who I am.

Thank you that You have given me specific gifts and abilities which are necessary for everyone in the whole body, in order for us all to grow and mature.

Holy Spirit, please help me to be open and responsive to the encouragement of others, and may I be an encouragement and help to them as well.

Amen.

INTERACTIVE SEVEN - VALUED TREASURE

We are not just needed, we are valued and precious to our God.

When Jesus went to the cross, the great joy which he anticipated ahead of him, was the thought of all the children who would come into God's kingdom, through his death and resurrection (Heb.12:2). Jesus came into the world to seek and to save what was lost (Lk.19:10). Just like the man in the parable in Matthew's gospel (Mt.13:44), Jesus looked for treasure, and He found us.

PRECIOUS JEWELS

In the Bible, the LORD uses the picture of jewels to symbolize how precious and valued we are.

For example, the high priest in Israel carried a breast-piece, set with twelve different, precious jewels, together representing the people of God. Each precious jewel had once been hidden in rock, but had then been found, cut and polished. What had once been in darkness, was now displayed in all its glory, on the high priest's breast-piece. Like those precious jewels, every one of us is valued and precious to God – royal jewels, cut carefully, in order to shine in many different directions and looking amazingly lovely.

We may have gone through some awful moments in our lives and feel quite rough round the edges, but the Lord is shaping and forming us up for display, as His wonderful treasure for all eternity.

Describe an experience in your life of being hidden, and then found, shaped and restored. Or what would you imagine that experience might be like?

_____

_____

_____

_____

_____

_____

_____

_____

_____

_____

_____

_____

_____

_____

_____

God shows us how much we are valued in a story
Jesus tells us in Luke's gospel.

Read Luke 15:11-32
How did the returning son feel by the end of the
story?

_____

_____

_____

_____

Read the following poem. Pick out a line or phrase
that encourages you that God values you for who
you are.

Hidden Treasure

Cleaning, polishing and restoring;

God sees the hidden treasure in us,

Others may only see rubbish

But He is the antique guy-

He sees what is hidden.

When the enemy tells you, "You're worthless!"

God looks inside you and sees hidden treasure.

When you put Him on the throne of your life,

He'll help you to overcome your past,

Resist temptation,

Break through your self-imposed limitations,

And start accepting that

In His eyes, you have great worth.

The divine nature is in me!

I am someone who is being transformed

Into His likeness.

I am an item that just needs to be cleaned,

Polished and restored,

In order to shine out Your glory anew.

Mary Bain July 2008

Which line or phrase did you pick and why?

_____

_____

_____

_____

_____

_____

_____

_____

_____

_____

PRAYER

Thank you, dear Lord. You have pulled me out of some very dark places and episodes, at different times in my life, and here I am standing before you, loved, embraced and valued as Your son. Amen.

INTERACTIVE EIGHT - A TEAM MISSION

Even when we are on individual assignments, we are still contributing to the bigger mission plan of God. Jesus has His team for us to work with. There are other team members to discover as we step out with Him!

'MIGHTY MEN'

Team can be unexpected - God brings out from the woodwork all sorts of people with whom He wants us to connect. They may not be our natural choices. As we step out with Jesus, we may be in for some surprises.

For example, when David was at the Cave of Adullam, on the run from King Saul, all sorts of people gathered round him. We read, *'All those who were in distress, or in debt, or discontented gathered around him and he became their leader'* (1 Sam.22:2).

They look like a very motley group. And yet, later on, in 1 Chronicles, chapter 11, they are described as a team of 'mighty men'! What happened in between? In the interim, God had been at work in all of their lives and made an amazing difference! His transforming power can make all the difference in our lives too.

Read 1 Corinthians 6:9-11 and also 1 Corinthian 1:26. List the types of people in Corinth that had heard the gospel and become believers.

_____

_____

_____

_____

_____

_____

_____

_____

_____

_____

It is clear that God is not fazed by what we look like, when we begin our journey with Him. He doesn't mind at all what others might consider unpromising material! He calls each one of us by name, with the faith to believe that we will become all He wants us to be.

VISIONARY NAMES

I love the meanings of people's names. They are usually very encouraging, and a good word over their lives. God loves each one of us and knows us by name. Your name may often reflect a God-given vision of who you are, or a promise from God for you to ponder on. My own name, Robert (Bob for short) has been a great source of inspiration for me. It can be understood to mean 'Bright flame', and God has shown me its applicability in different experiences I have been through. My parents may have had all sorts of reasons why they picked it, but I believe God ultimately directed their thinking. Of course, some names have been foolishly or maliciously given, and in some circumstances, you might ask the Lord to show you a new name, by which you would like to be called. Let Him have the final say.

What about your name? Search on the internet the meaning of your name and write below what you came up with.

_____

_____

_____

_____

_____

_____

Pray about what your name might indicate.
Does the meaning of your name encourage you in any situation you are currently experiencing, or one from the past?

_____

_____

_____

_____

_____

_____

_____

_____

_____

_____

_____

_____

_____

The names of the different 'mighty men' listed in 1 Chronicles chapter 11 are full of good meanings. What an encouragement to David, as this motley crew arrived at the Cave of Adullam to join him, and told him their names.

Here are some of them (1 Ch.11:26-30)

- *Asahel - 'God is the One who fashions us, who makes us who we are'*
- *Elhanan - 'He is the One who graciously gives'*
- *Helez - 'the LORD is our strength'*
- *Ira - 'the One who is attentive and watchful over us'*
- *Abiezer - 'the Father of our support and help'*
- *Sibbecai - 'the LORD who sustains us'*
- *Ilia - 'the One who is exalted'*
- *Heled - 'the One who sees the whole of life, the big picture'*
- *Maharai - 'He is not tardy but swift on our behalf'*

Because David had a prophetic gift, he would have been encouraged, as he sensed that God was going to change these oddball people, so that their characters reflected the names that they had been given. God was making them into an amazing, supportive team.

Choose one of the names above that encourages you with its particular truth about the character of God, in the context of a team working together. Why did you choose this one?

_____

_____

_____

_____

_____

_____

_____

_____

_____

God also wants to encourage us in a different way, through the names of these 'mighty men'. He wants us to believe that team members may themselves be ...

- gracious like Elhanan,
- strong like Helez,
- watchful like Ira,
- helpful and supportive like Abiezer,
- seeing the bigger picture like Heled,
- swift and quick when it was needed like Maharai

What characteristic especially appeals to you if you had to pick out just one from this list for a fellow team member?
Why did you choose this one? (a difficult choice!)

_____

_____

_____

_____

_____

_____

_____

_____

_____

_____

When Jesus saw Simon, He gave him the name, Peter – the rock (John 1:42). As He got to know James and John, He called them Sons of Thunder, perhaps because of their bold personalities (Mk.3:17). The first apostles gave a man named Joseph, the name Barnabas, which means Son of Encouragement (Acts 4:36). Regardless of your actual name, we all carry characteristics about us that others, by faith, may see and appreciate. Sometimes people may call us by a new name, or a nickname that reflects a characteristic that they particularly like about us.

What name do you think you might be called, by someone who <u>appreciates you</u>?
Why?

_____

_____

_____

_____

_____

_____

_____

_____

_____

_____

_____

_____

Who has God put into your life, to help you fulfill everything He wants to do in and through you – making up your very own 'mighty men' team?

_____

_____

_____

_____

_____

_____

_____

_____

_____

_____

_____

_____

_____

A similar question to ask in reverse:-
For whom do you believe God is calling you to be 'team' at this time? (They may not be the same people as you listed earlier.)

_____

_____

_____

_____

_____

_____

_____

_____

_____

_____

_____

_____

_____

It is time for us to follow the example of Jesus, and serve one another in whatever way is needed, and not just think of our own personal interests. Ultimately, God is the head of the team, and we want to hear from Him as to who we do life with.

PRAYER

Lord, however we see ourselves, may we seek to be a blessing to others with whom you have called us to walk.

Jesus, please show us how we fit into Your team. It may be a big step, but today we say that we are willing to walk with others and not keep ourselves to ourselves. Amen.

If possible pray for one another in groups.

INTERACTIVE NINE - TEAM PICTURES

The following three pictures convey some different aspects and ways of understanding 'team'. We have found them helpful to stimulate discussion about what 'team' is, and how we can encourage and build team together. We pray that God will also speak to you as you study them.We have chosen the following three pictures believing they will convey to you some different aspects about team. We pray that God will speak to you through them.

Look at the pictures carefully.
What do you think God may be saying to you about 'team' through each picture?
(You can see colour versions of these pictures in the resources section of welcomenetwork.org)

A PALLETTE OF PAINTS

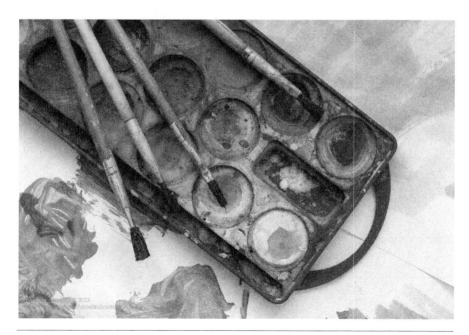

FISHERMEN PULLING IN A NET

_____

_____

_____

_____

_____

_____

THE INTER-WOVEN, MULTI-COLOURED BASKET

Here are some short notes about team to add to your own.

A PALLETTE OF PAINTS – NOTES

It's all very messy. There has been a work going on. Different colours coming together to make something new, that couldn't be done by just a single colour. I love the fact it's messy. Having raised seven children in a small ex-council house, there was a messy dynamic equilibrium between what children were bringing down the stairs, (toys), and what adults were taking back up the stairs, (also toys), let alone the laundry going up and down the stairs as well!

Where there are no oxen the manger is clean. But where there are oxen, there is a harvest. (Prov 14:4)

We need to accept that teams are <u>messy</u>, yet we hope that God's fruitful plan is still happening

We are more likely to hear the mind of the Lord, as <u>we bring our different personalities</u>, like different colours, to the table.

'just as iron sharpens iron, so one man sharpens another' (Pr.27:17).

When a rich palette of paints is <u>gathered together</u>, wonderful paintings can start to happen! Together Everyone Achieves More – T.E.A.M.

'Team' is a creative place to be!

FISHERMEN PULLING IN A NET - NOTES

To pull the net successfully, the team have all had to decide to <u>get into position</u>, and to <u>be single-focussed</u> on the task that they have to do. There is a direction to their energy and effort.

We do need to identify what the Lord is saying to us about <u>working together</u>, so that we don't dissipate our energy. It may be that we need to let some things go in order to focus our energy and attention on a particular task.

THE INTER-WOVEN, MULTI-COLOURED BASKET - NOTES

The variety and the care in which it has been put together stands out. Singly, we see just strands of material, but put together they become a container that can hold something. We need to realise that God can put us together in a way that will help us to further the Kingdom of God.

The basket is unfinished – there is an ongoing work, that we get to be a part of for a season. It is humbling and helpful to realise that we are not indispensable. When we move on God is not wringing His hands, saying 'Oh my goodness, what are we going to do now?' because God has a way of bringing together the people He needs to get His work done.

I wouldn't have a clue in the Art and Craft department, so if I was given this basket, the only way it would get finished would have to be God.

'we are woven together in the fabric of God's love'
(Col.2:2 Msg version)

REVIEW 1

Look back and review the different Sentness interactives in this first section on Purpose and Direction. Write down one or two thoughts from each.

Sentness – Interactive 1

_____

_____

_____

_____

_____

Positioned by the Spirit – Interactive 2

_____

_____

_____

_____

_____

_____

Opening Doors – Interactive 3

_____

_____

_____

_____

_____

Stick with Jesus – Interactive 4

_____

_____

_____

_____

_____

Stepping out – Interactive 5

_____

_____

_____

All Needed – Interactive 6

All Valued – Interactive 7

A Team Mission – Interactive 8

_____

_____

_____

_____

_____

_____

Team Pictures – Interactive 9

_____

_____

_____

_____

_____

PART TWO
COMMUNITY &
COMMUNICATIONS

Building Healthy Relationships

INTERACTIVE TEN - COMMUNITY AND COMMUNICATIONS

'Just as each of us has one body with many members, and these members do not all have the same function, so in Christ we who are many form one body, and each member belongs to all the others.' (Rom.12:4-5)

First, there is 'me' and then there is 'us'. As soon as we come into relationship with God, we discover we are also called into a relationship with other believers, as well. Our relationship together is described as being members of the body of Jesus Christ. So, if when we think about 'us' in terms of a community of believers, 'the body' is one important word to consider. But there are also other words in the Bible which describe what it means for people, as believers, to be in relationship with one another. We are calling these words 'community words'.

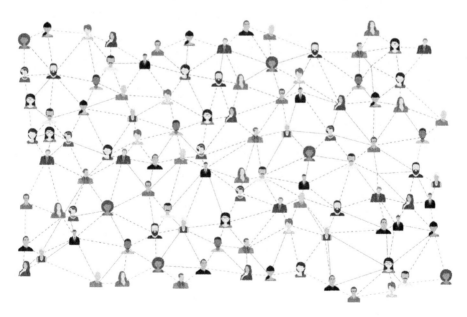

Communications are at the heart of any community.

Below are listed some 'community' words, which describe our relationship as believers, labeled A to G, and a list of qualities and characteristics which we might associate with them.

Pick at least one quality or characteristic for each community word. (There can be more than one characteristic for each community word, and there are no set answers).

If you are in a group, share your choices with others in the group afterwards.

COMMUNITY WORDS

A KINGDOM _____

B BRIDE _____

C BUILDING _____

D BODY _____

E FAMILY _____

F RIVER _____

G FEAST _____

QUALITIES AND CHARACTERISTICS

Welcome
Order
Generosity
Stability
Hospitality
Joy
Companionship
Relationships
Strength
Healing
Intimacy
Peace
Beauty
Connectedness
Eating Together
Belonging
Refreshing
Celebration
Food
God's presence
Friendship
Shelter

Out of the following 'community' words, choose the best word to put next to each of the Bible verses;- Kingdom, Bride, Building, Body, Family, River and Feast.

'...For we are the temple of the Living God...' (2 Cor.6:16)

_____

'Many will come from the east and the west, and will take their places at the feast with Abraham, Isaac and Jacob in the Kingdom of Heaven' (Matthew 8:11)

_____

'Husbands love your wives, just as Christ loved the church and gave Himself up for her' (Eph 5:25)

_____

'You are all sons of God through faith in Christ Jesus' (Gal 3:26)

_____

'The angel showed me the river of the water of life, as clear as crystal, flowing from the throne of God and of the Lamb down the middle of the great street of the city...' (Rev. 22:2-3)

_____

'Now you are the body of Christ and each one of you is a part of it' (1 Cor.12:27)

_____

'You are no longer foreigners and aliens but fellow-citizens with God's people...' (Eph.2:19)

COMMUNICATIONS

Communications and connections are at the heart of any community, and help to build the healthy relationships that God wants between us as believers.

Without communications, our relationships with others can become strained and fragmented, and the qualities and characteristics of healthy community don't happen as well as they should.

In New Testament times, communications were done by letter, or by a personal visit, or simply by sending another person on your behalf. Telephone calls, texts, emails and social media now provide additional opportunities to communicate. Connections are being made across the whole church, all the time, through this stream of communication, and this shouldn't be taken for granted. Like rabbits in a warren, digging underground tunnels to connect with one another, a lot of communication needs to go on across the church, in an often unseen but vital way in order to build healthy relationships.

CIRCLES OF COMMUNICATIONS

In principle, God would want us to have good communications with anybody and everybody. However, realistically there are particular circles of people He has sent us to, and with whom He will especially want us to connect.

With which circles of people do you think it is <u>especially important</u> for you to keep in good communications at this present time? (whether believers or not)

_____

_____

_____

_____

_____

_____

_____

_____

_____

_____

_____

_____

'RABBIT WARREN' COMMUNICATIONS!

WHO CONNECTS with WHO in this NETWORK?
Using the following Bible verses,

1 Thess 3:2   Eph 6:21-22   Col 4:7-9
Titus 3:12-13   Acts 21:18-19   Rom 16:1-2

Can you work out which person is connecting with which other person (or persons), and also sometimes asking them to connect with someone else later: Draw straight lines to show the connections.

PAUL   PHOEBE

                                        TITUS

              ONESIMUS   ROMANS

                                        JAMES

                                COLOSSIANS

              TYCHICUS

              TIMOTHY   THESSALONIANS

              APOLLOS

                                        EPHESIANS
              ZENAS

(see page 201 for our attempt at mapping the rabbit warren)

A COMMUNICATIONS CHECK LIST

This is a short list of some of the helpful communication wisdom we can learn as we read through the New Testament letters.

> Remember everyone is precious and special to God
> Be friendly – greet people!
> Share your news and the things that matter to you.
> Share your experiences
> Clear up misunderstandings
> Communicate arrangements clearly.
> Encourage others to communicate

John says, *'I have much to write to you, but I do not want to do so with pen and ink. I hope to see you soon, and we will talk face to face* (3 Jn.13-14).

INTERACTIVE ELEVEN - ENCOURAGEMENTS

'When we could stand it no longer…we sent Timothy… to strengthen and encourage you… to find out about your faith' (1 Thess.3:1-5).

We are social creatures, born into a setting with a growing circle of relationships. People need to hear and receive one anothers' news. There are personal events going on in all our lives – people are unwell, family members are getting married, children are being born. In God's eyes, everyone is special and what is happening in their lives is important to Him. Our communications should keep that thought in mind.

'Tychicus…will tell you everything so that you also may know how I am and what I am doing. I am sending him to you for this very purpose that you may know how we are…' (Eph.6:21-22).

Mary and I spend a lot of time connecting with people, either individually, or in gatherings and forums. Wonderful, long-lasting relationships have been built over cups of coffee, emails, telephone and zoom calls. Let us seek to be encouraging in the different settings in which we find ourselves.

FOUNDATIONAL EXPERIENCES

There are certain key foundational experiences which have shaped our lives. Sharing them can be of benefit to others. There will be occasions when God particularly arranges for you to have a conversation with someone, in which the experiences you share are just what they need to hear. We need to stay sensitive to these opportunities in order to be a blessing and encouragement to others.

One major foundational experience is how we came to know Jesus. Everyone one of us has a 'Jesus' story to share.

Spend some time reflecting on your own 'Jesus' story - how you came to know Him, and what that felt like.
What are some of the foundational moments in your story? Were there some key people involved in it?

_____

_____

_____

_____

_____

_____

_____

_____

_____

_____

_____

_____

_____

Who might you consider sharing your foundational story with?

_____

_____

_____

SHARING WITH OTHERS OUR ENCOURAGING TIMES WITH JESUS

We are all unique, and so our prayer times will not be the same for you as for someone else. When you meet with Jesus, it's good to express your love for Him in your own way, so if you're a singer, sing, if you're a dancer, dance, if you draw things do that; if you write poetry or any other form of expression, do it! Listen quietly, or shout out loud! God loves you just as you are! Communicating to others our own experiences with Jesus, can encourage them in their times with Him.

Read Luke 10:38-42

In this passage, Mary has a wonderful experience of being with Jesus as she

LISTENS

Is STILL

RECEIVES His love

LOOKS into His face

ENJOYS His presence

Is NOT DISTRACTED

Jesus answered, '...*few things are needed – indeed only one. Mary has chosen what is better...*' Luke 10:42

'It's alright, Martha – you can sit at Jesus' feet too'

What is ONE way or ONE experience of coming closer to Jesus which you could share to encourage others?

If you are in a small group, share your thoughts.

_____

_____

_____

_____

_____

Write down any personal examples where you were part of the following scenarios involving communications.

1. Helpful words which woke someone (or yourself) up to God's purposes and plans. As a result, that person (or yourself) reconnected with God's purpose for their life.

_____

_____

_____

_____

_____

_____

_____

_____

2. God's words of life in teaching or prophecy made all the difference in a particular situation, or to a particular decision you were making.

_____

_____

_____

_____

_____

_____

_____

3. God used a personal experience as a helpful example for others to hear.

_____

_____

_____

_____

_____

_____

_____

4. Prayer and support were given, to those on ministry assignments to places elsewhere in the world.

_____

_____

_____

_____

_____

_____

5. A <u>mutual</u> giving and receiving of words of support and encouragement happened.
'I long to see you... that you and I may be mutually encouraged by each other's faith' (Rom.1:12).

_____

_____

_____

_____

_____

_____

6. Words spoken (or written) in the past were recalled and helped someone, (or yourself), to live in a way that pleased God. As Peter writes,

'I have written both of [my letters] as <u>reminders</u> to stimulate you to wholesome thinking. I want you to <u>recall</u> the words spoken in the past by the holy prophets and the command given by our Lord and Saviour through your apostles' **(2 Pet.3:1-2).**

_____

_____

_____

_____

_____

_____

_____

_____

_____

It's good to intentionally recall the good things which have kept us on track – the words from God which have been spoken over us in prayer and prophecy.

'Do not let any unwholesome talk come out of your mouths, but <u>only</u> what is <u>helpful for building others up</u> according to their needs, that it may benefit those who listen' (Eph.4:29).

Name one person you can support and encourage through your communications and connections today. In what ways might you do this?

_____

_____

_____

_____

_____

_____

_____

_____

_____

_____

INTERACTIVE TWELVE - DISTURBED

Sometimes our conversations with others can disturb them. This can be good if the things in which people are involved have lost their relevancy. There are occasions when our words will be used by God to bring people back to His purpose, from bad habits, or just regular and comfortable routines.

How might moles illustrate this ?

_____

_____

_____

_____

_____

Why might archaeologists find moles useful?

What spiritual lesson might we draw from this?

_____

_____

_____

_____

_____

_____

_____

ROUTINES AND BAD HABITS

Can you think of any occasions when someone has either directly, or indirectly, brought about changes in your routines or habits?

This could be through a conversation, seeing their example, listening to a talk or reading a book.

Write down a couple of examples.

_____

_____

_____

_____

_____

COLLABORATIVE THINKING

One word that can often be a disturbing challenge to our usual ways of interacting with others is the word 'collaborative'. In terms of our mission together to proclaim the gospel, it expresses how much God desires us to work in unity with other believers.

Look up, online or otherwise, and write down the definition of 'Collaborative'.

_____

_____

_____

_____

_____

The Lausanne statement says, '*It takes the whole church to take the whole gospel to the whole city*'.

How 'collaborative' is our thinking?
How far are we <u>willing</u> to build relationships with other Christians for the sake of the gospel?
What might stop us?

_____

_____

_____

_____

_____

_____

_____

_____

_____

_____

_____

_____

'What missional things can we do together with others, which will reach the area?'

_____

_____

_____

_____

_____

_____

_____

_____

_____

_____

_____

_____

Write what Psalm 133:1 says:-

_____

_____

_____

_____

PRAYER

Lord, may we seek to be a blessing to others in all our conversations and other communications. Give us the wise words to say in every situation whether pleasant or difficult.

Amen

If possible, pray for one another in groups.

REVIEW 2

Look back and review the different Sentness interactives in this second section on Community and Communications. Write down one or two thoughts from each.

Community and Communications – Interactive 10

_____

_____

_____

_____

_____

Encouragements – Interactive 11

_____

_____

_____

_____

Disturbed – Interactive 12

PART THREE
MOTHERS &
FATHERS

How God wants us to grow up and become mothers and
fathers to those around us.

INTERACTIVE THIRTEEN - THE PARENTING OF GOD

'Our Father in Heaven... Your Kingdom come, Your will be done, on earth as it is in Heaven'

God is in the parenting business.

GOD OUR FATHER

The clue is in the name! Jesus, again and again, in the gospels refers to God as his Father, and taught his first disciples to pray, addressing God as *'Our Father in Heaven'*. Father God is in the parenting business. He is the ultimate parent and we are His children.

How does John say we can become children of God? (John 1:12-13)

_____

_____

_____

_____

_____

_____

_____

_____

What is the primary feeling that is conveyed in this picture of a dad with his two young daughters? What do you think are God's feelings towards <u>you</u>?

_____

_____

_____

_____

_____

_____

_____

_____

_____

_____

_____

_____

_____

_____

_____

_____

_____

A PARENTING PASSAGE

There is a passage in Paul's letter to the Ephesians which I call God's parenting passage (Eph.3:14 to 4:16). It starts with Paul the apostle kneeling in prayer before Father God, *'from whom his whole family in heaven and on earth derives its name'*, and finishes with a vision of God's people grown up, equipped and mature. In between, a process is described, which is, in its essence, a parenting one. Father God is raising His children to be adults. We are born, by the Holy Spirit, into God's family, but He isn't leaving any of us as spiritual babies.

Within this parenting passage, there are five ascension gifts listed (as they are sometimes called). What are they? (Eph 4:11)

a)_____

b)_____

c)_____

d)_____

e)_____

What do they <u>collectively</u> do? (Eph 4:12-13)

_____

_____

_____

_____

_____

_____

_____

_____

The five Ascension gifts are people, and are at the heart of God's parenting process. In this process He is using 'Ascension gift' people to directly, or indirectly help each of us to grow up. These are key people who carry qualities which can uniquely help us, not only to mature but also to become a blessing to those around us.

KEY PEOPLE IN OUR LIVES

Mary and I have had many experiences in which we have been helped by key people whom God has brought our way, whether they were 'Ascension' gifts or not. They were people who gave us valuable input, at important moments or seasons in our lives.

For example, we became Christians through a student mission group, when we were at university. However, we had all sorts of issues fitting in with them. Fortunately, one of Bob's friends saw the problem, and created a group where we were able to grow. He didn't mind us asking questions, and opened us up to some of the amazing ways God can speak through the Bible.

Later, when we were young parents, an older couple, with three children, kindly gave us some time to learn from them practical skills on how to be more organized in our routines, and how to handle our domestic finances better. They also encouraged us, by their example, in praying together as a couple.

For a few minutes, think about the key people whom God has used to provide valuable input at important moments in your life. This could be in the form of encouragement, practical advice or godly wisdom.

Write down something about <u>one</u> of those key people.
If you are in a group you could share with others.

_____

_____

_____

_____

_____

_____

_____

_____

_____

_____

Prayer

Thank you, Lord, for the different key people you have brought into my life.

Amen.

INTERACTIVE FOURTEEN - THE FIVE-FOLD GIFTED PARENT

We can learn something about how the five-fold 'Ascension' gifts help to bring us to maturity, from looking at how good parents raise their children.

PARENTS REFLECT GOD'S IMAGE

Jesus pulls on the comparison between human parents and our Heavenly Father. He shows, for example, the depth of God's love for us in the Parable of the Lost Son in Luke chapter fifteen, which we looked at earlier in Interactive Seven on Valued Treasure.

Jesus also talks about God in fatherly terms in other passages. What does he say His Heavenly Father gives to us in these verses?

Matthew 7:11?

_____

_____

_____

Luke 11:13?

_____

_____

_____

Paul also had a parenting heart towards others around him. Read 1Thessalonians 2:7, 11 - 12. What does he say about himself in...?

Verse 7?

_____

_____

_____

Verse 11 - 12?

_____

_____

_____

_____

Good parents also image our Father God in the family life they try to create. God's parenting heart is shown in the different ways in which they relate with their children. We discover that parents naturally draw on the same parenting process as our Father God does, using the different ascension gift qualities to help their children to grow into all He has planned and shaped them to be.

Parents feed and nurture their children i.e. they pastor them; they also teach them; they share their faith with them - evangelism; they declare prophetic words over them and also want their children to hear for themselves words from the Lord. So what about the apostolic qualities parents are exercising.

HOW ARE PARENTS ALSO BEING APOSTOLIC?

Here are a few thoughts:-

1) PURPOSE AND CALLING

Parents want the best for their children. They want to help them to understand that God has a purpose and calling on their lives, and gifts for them to develop.

For example, we recognized quite early on that our eldest son, David was really good at art and painting. He was always wanting to draw things, so we did our best to encourage him in this, buying him special art materials, and when a Christmas card competition came up, we encouraged him to enter it and he won first prize. Later on, he went to Art College and got a degree and now he's doing well as a self-employed illustrator in Bristol.

Good parents will always want to encourage and draw out the gifts that they see in their children.

2) AN ADVENTURE OF DISCOVERY

Parents take their children on an exciting adventure of discovery of the world around them, and their place in it. They introduce them to new experiences, in which they find out more about themselves.

Mary remembers that when she was a little girl, she actually found a wild strawberry plant on a bank beside the road. She pulled it up, and decided to take it home, because she wanted to plant it and grow some strawberries. Her Dad, who was a great gardener, encouraged her, and gave her a patch of ground. He also showed her how the strawberry plant puts out runners to make more plants. She thinks that this is one big reason why she enjoys gardening so much today.

3) BUILDING AND ESTABLISHING

Parents not only help their children understand their purpose in life, but they also help to build and establish them in it. We had a season when we regularly took one of our sons along to play football in a team. Other ones of our children were taken to choir days and bird watching weekends.

4) GIVING AN OVERVIEW

It is important for parents to give their children an overview, to help them stay true to God's plan – the bigger picture. They are called into His Kingdom and glory (1 Thess.2:12).

When we look at how parents raise their children, we start to get a better understanding of what our Heavenly Father is doing through the Ascension gift people in our lives.

THANK YOU!

We might not all have had good parents, and even the best parents have had their bad moments. However, there are some things we can be thankful for, whether through our biological parents, or those who have been 'Mum and Dad' figures in our lives.

Pause for a moment and reflect on what you are thankful for - something you have learnt while growing up from a significant parent figure, our mum, dad or someone else. It doesn't have to be a childhood memory – it can be a more recent adult memory.
Have a thankful pause for the next five minutes
(you may want to write something down)

_____

_____

_____

_____

_____

INTERACTIVE FIFTEEN - MOTHERS AND FATHERS IN OUR COMMUNITY

GOD WANTS US ALL TO BE 'PARENTS'

God's desire for all of us is to grow into maturity, and to become 'mothers and fathers' to those around us - in church life, our communities, schools and places of work. Just as there have been key people who have helped us, God's plan is that we mature and be available to help others. The world is desperately in need of fathers and mothers! There are millions of people who have orphan hearts, who feel lonely and isolated or are in disruptive and dysfunctional family situations. We don't have to go around calling ourselves 'mothers and fathers', but our aim and heart attitude should aspire to reflect our Heavenly Father in how we are with others.

Each ascension gift has its unique part to play in developing parenting qualities within us, as they shape us in the apostolic, prophetic, evangelistic, pastoral and teaching ways of living and interacting with others. As we allow ourselves to be shaped and transformed, we can start to influence and bless our communities as 'mother and father' figures.

Which 'ascension gift' qualities are at work in the following things we might find ourselves doing within our communities?

Our responses will be either
a) apostolic b) prophetic c) evangelistic d) pastoral e) teaching or f) all of them!

Showing practical care _____

Being a voice of wisdom _____

Encouraging someone to go for their dream _____

Being a stable presence of peace _____

Speaking out a timely word _____

Praying with someone to become a Christian _____

Showing God's love _____

If you are in a group, you can compare your answers with one another.

There are 'ascension gift' qualities of being a parent figurethat God wants us to display in particular settings. It could be in the church; it could be in the way we are parenting our own children; it could be in our communities, and for some it might even be a way of parenting a nation. We all have different capacities, settings and contexts in which the Lord might ask us to express His heavenly parenting qualities to others.

If you have never thought about this before, it might be a new idea, to think about your neighbourhood, your street, your community in terms of God having appointed you to be, in some way, a 'parent' there. Whatever the setting, our home area, a work place or online, God will show us how to express our own unique calling.

In what ways do you think God might want you to be a 'mother or father figure' in your community?
If you have a pastoral heart for example, this might primarily be as a caring presence.
(if you are with others, you may want to discuss this question in groups of twos or threes).

_____

_____

_____

_____

_____

_____

_____

_____

_____

_____

GOD IS ABLE

How can this amazing maturing into parenthood come about? It is beyond us to figure it out! We must humbly come to God and ask Him to help us.

Paul kneels and prays, *'that out of God's glorious riches, He may strengthen you with power through His Spirit in your inner being...'* (Eph.3:16-19).

Paul then immediately encourages us with these words.
'Now to Him who is able to give us immeasurably more than all we ask or imagine according to His power that is at work within us - to Him be glory in the church and in Christ Jesus throughout all generations, for ever and ever. Amen.' (Ephesians 3:20)

A THANKFUL RESPONSE

As children of God, we have a growing self-awareness of His parenting work in our lives. The longer we have known Him, the more we have come to appreciate the different ways in which He has been at work, the different people He has brought into our lives and His end goal for us - *'to be filled to the measure of all His fullness'* (Eph.3:19). He has been shaping us and working with us over many years, bringing us to maturity, and all for our benefit, and for the benefit of others. We begin to realise the extent of the process that has been going on, and are very thankful to God our Father.

PRAYER
Father, thank you for Your amazing love towards each one of us, as Your children. Please show us how to be 'mother and father' figures. Lead us as we grow in this, and become a blessing to the people around us. Amen.

REVIEW 3

Look back and review the different Sentness interactives in this third section on Mothers and Fathers. Write down one or two thoughts from each.

The Parenting of God – Interactive 13

_____

_____

_____

_____

_____

The Five-fold Parent – Interactive 14

_____

_____

_____

_____

_____

Mothers and Fathers in our community – Interactive 15

PART FOUR
DEEPER
WITH JESUS

Getting ready for the big day!

INTERACTIVE SIXTEEN - DEEPER WITH JESUS

'You have stolen my heart, my sister, my bride; you have stolen my heart with one glance of your eyes, with one jewel of your necklace'
(Song of Songs 4:9)

THE VISION OF THE BRIDE

In Ephesians 5:27, we are described as a radiant Bride being presented to Christ *'without stain or wrinkle or any other blemish but holy and blameless.'*

There is a wonderful picture that is a foreshadowing of the Bride of Christ in Psalm 45:10-17. The royal bride, on her wedding day, is described in these terms, *'all-glorious is the princess within her chamber. Her gown is inter-woven with gold, in embroidered garments she is led to the king. The king is enthralled by her beauty.'* The author of Hebrews quotes this psalm as being about the Son of God (Heb.1:8-9), so it is not fanciful to understand the royal bride as being the church as well.

When we understand our relationship with Christ in terms of a Bride being wed to her Bridegroom, then our growing into maturity is really all about knowing and experiencing Jesus more and more closely in this way. Just like a husband and a wife in marriage, each one of us is called on this personal journey of going deeper with Jesus.

In Psalm forty-five, the royal bride is told to listen and consider these instructions. What are they?

Verse 10

_____

_____

_____

_____

Verse 11

_____

_____

_____

_____

_____

_____

_____

Similar thoughts are expressed by Paul in his letters to the Philippians and Ephesians.

'…One thing I do; Forgetting what is behind and straining towards what is ahead, I press on towards the goal to win the prize for which God has called me heavenwards in Christ Jesus' (Phil.3:13-14)

'…the wife must honour and respect her husband' (Eph.5:33)

God wants us to keep our eyes on the vision He has for us, and not get distracted by the things that have gone on in our past. He has called us into a new relationship, which must now be the focus of our attention.

A JOURNEY OF INTIMACY

The journey of getting to know Jesus begins when we first respond and give our hearts to Him.

However, as the years go by, we can easily get sidetracked - we may get too busy and start depending on other people, or other things, rather than depending on Jesus. We can lose the freshness and excitement that we enjoyed at the beginning of our journey, when we first knew Him. We then discover how much our Bridegroom cherishes our relationship with Him.

He starts to draw us, and woo us back to Himself. All the way through our lives He does this, pulling our heart strings and desiring us to come into His presence. He brings us back to our senses and resets our hearts to how they are meant to be.

LISTENING EXERCISE – SONG OF SONGS

On our journey into intimacy, if we really want to hear Jesus, our Bridegroom, calling us to meet Him in the secret place, the best book to go to in the Bible is the Song of Songs. Before we look at a passage from this book, let us pause, be still and pray this short prayer.

PRAYER

Lord Jesus, help us as we listen to Your words, to hear what You are saying, and to become more aware of Your presence in our lives.
Amen

Read through the following passage from the Song of Songs. Read it slowly, pausing every so often. Then read it through again two or three more times.

As you read, LISTEN, and imagine that Jesus is speaking to you.

"My beloved spoke, and said to me:
Rise up, my love, my fair one,
And come away.
For lo, the winter is past,
The rain is over and gone,
The flowers appear on the earth;
The time of singing has come,
And the voice of the turtledove
Is heard in our land.

The fig tree puts forth her green figs,

And the vines with the tender grapes
Give a good smell,
Rise up, my love, my fair one,
And come away!

O my dove, in the clefts of the rock
In the secret places of the cliff
Let me see your face
Let me hear your voice
For your voice is sweet,
And your face is lovely"

(Song of Songs 2:10-14)

Did a particular phrase or thought stand out for you, or touch your heart?
Keep thinking about this word, feeling, or new thought.
You may want to pray quietly, or respond to Jesus out loud.
Finally, write down your thoughts or your own prayer here.

_____

_____

_____

_____

_____

_____

_____

_____

_____

_____

_____

_____

_____

_____

_____

_____

_____

A DATE IN THE DIARY

There is a future wedding date, to which we are all looking
forward, described in the final chapters of the Bible. The church
is coming to her own wedding; she has been invited to *'the
wedding supper of the Lamb'* (Rev.19:9).

Mary

Together with His Father and the Holy Spirit

The Bridegroom, Jesus Christ & His lovely Bride,

the Church

Request the honour of your presence

at their WEDDING...

"COME

FOLLOW

ME!"

and afterwards

at the Marriage Supper of the LAMB.

RSVP

The following poem was written a few years ago, when we were moving house. It tells the story (with a bit of poetic license) of how I met Jesus over forty years ago.

THE INVITATION

I found it a few days ago
Sorting out things for the move
I had forgotten how big it was
Edged in gold
White card, hand written
Beautiful, carefully crafted,
My personal invitation-
To the Wedding.
Wrapped around it, even still
The soft tissue paper
I had kept, as it had been then,
Covered in hearts, and still carrying
The sweet, lingering perfume
Of His presence...
I pulled it off
And held the card in my hand...

The years rolled away
I was a student again
Sitting on my bed,
A Sunday evening after Mass,
Alone.
My heart aching within me
I had been learning something hard to handle,
It made me feel lonely and afraid,
The man I thought was in love with me
Wanted me to be someone else.

The scene moved forward;
I was drinking coffee
In Bob's new room,

Chatting and laughing,
Feeling excited again
My heart beating fast
As our eyes met and we shared
About the book
He'd been reading that week
Could it really be true?

Then, another scene;
A conversation with Bob's friend, a Christian,
"Did I really know Jesus?" was the question;
"Did I know what He had done for me?"
I thought I did;
I answered all the questions correctly,
Except the last.
Why had no one said this before?
"Had I really given Him my heart?"

Back in my own room again
I read through the leaflet
Bob's friend had given me
It made such perfect sense;
Every word spoke hope and healing
Into my empty, aching heart.
I had been looking for a man
To fill the void inside,
Give me affirmation,
To love me, just as I am.
I discovered Jesus,
Loving me completely, totally,
Even before I was born!
Dying, just for me;
It went far and beyond the love of a man!
Nothing more was needed;
I prayed a simple prayer
And opened my heart to Him...

And that was when I received the Invitation;
As I slept that night,
Jesus walked into my room.
I felt His presence,
His touch on my forehead,
His soft whisper of love,
"Now you are Mine."
In the morning I found the card
On my pillow,
My name written at the top
In gold, and below
Three simple words-
"Come, follow Me!"

And so the Invitation is definitely being packed
With all our belongings
As Bob and I move on today.
The joy found in following Jesus
Continues to grow.
And I know
It was the best decision I have ever made
To give my heart, and live my life,
Forever, with Him.

And yes, the Wedding is still to come,
And the Bridegroom is tenderly calling
To you, dear Reader;
Have you discovered your invitation yet?
He is waiting for you.

Mary Bain April 2017

The physical wedding invitation card referred to in the poem is poetic license, but the meeting with Jesus in my bedroom really did happen.

Now fill in your own name on the invitation!

Together with His Father and the Holy Spirit
The Bridegroom, Jesus Christ & His lovely Bride,
the Church
Request the honour of your presence
at their WEDDING...

"COME

FOLLOW

ME!"

and afterwards
at the Marriage Supper of the LAMB.

RSVP

INTERACTIVE SEVENTEEN - BEAUTY PREPARATIONS

'Let us rejoice and be glad and give Him glory for the wedding of the Lamb has come and His Bride has made herself ready.

(Revelation 19:7)

The Bride can be understood not just as a single person, but also as a corporate Bride – all of us, together in the Body of Jesus Christ.

What does Revelation 21:2 say about the Bride?

_____

_____

_____

_____

_____

_____

The city described in this passage isn't really about buildings, but is more like a network of relationships into which the Lord is calling us; with our Bridegroom, Jesus, at the centre of it. As believers, we are being prepared for a deep communion of relationships – with God, and with one another.

A DIVINE PREPARATION

Revelation 19:7 says that the Bride has made herself ready, but really the whole Trinity of God has been at work as well.

FATHER

The Bible passage, which we earlier named as the Parenting passage (Ephesians 3 and 4), describes how we are being brought through to maturity, but there is a bigger purpose in what is happening as well - the Father is preparing a beautiful Bride to present to His Son. In the same way that in the beginning, God presented Eve to Adam, as his wife, so now we have the Bride being presented, by the Father, to His Son Jesus. Our growth into maturity as Christians has this wonderful and amazing purpose!

JESUS

Jesus is also presenting us to Himself, as a radiant bride.

'Christ loved the church and gave Himself up for her to make her holy... and to present her to Himself as a radiant church, without stain or wrinkle or any other blemish, but holy and blameless'.
(Eph 5:25 - 27)

He has wooed us to Himself in a courtship, described in chapter after chapter of Song of Songs, pouring out words of love and invitation over His beloved. He invites us to come away with him, *'My lover spoke and said to me, Arise, my darling, my beautiful one, and come with me'* (SS.2:10).

The reason why Jesus came down to the earth was to rescue us, and to bring us to live with Himself forever. He has laid down his life for his Bride, *'Christ loved the church and gave Himself up for her'* (Eph.5:25).

HOLY SPIRIT

The Holy Spirit is also making us ready, by producing good fruit in us – in Galatians 5:22-23a there is a beautiful list of the sort of fruit coming out from within us, because of the Holy Spirit's presence in our life.

Very interestingly, the Holy Spirit can be described as an engagement ring. In Ephesians 1:13-14 and 2 Corinthians 1:22, we read about the Holy Spirit being a deposit, guaranteeing our inheritance. That word, 'deposit' (arrabon), can be translated 'engagement ring'. An engagement ring is the visible sign of a promise that a wedding is coming, but actually it is deeper than that, because the Holy Spirit is more than an outward promise – He also lives inside us, to help us to get ready for our wedding day.

In the final few verses of the Bible (Rev 22:17), the Holy Spirit is crying out together with the Bride, *'Come Lord Jesus'*.

THE ASCENSION GIFTS

The 'Ascension gift' people, described in Ephesians 4:11, are also helping in this preparation process of the Bride. The apostles, prophets, evangelists, pastors and teachers stand apart from the church for a moment, and fuss around us, tidying up this and that bit of the dress, while we stand in front of the mirror of the Word of God!

Paul as an apostle, for example, describes the Corinthian believers in these terms – *'I promised you to one husband, to Christ, so that I might present you as a pure virgin to him'* (2 Cor.11:2).

Through all these different people, God has been nurturing an atmosphere in which we are stirred up to grow in our love for Jesus, our Bridegroom. Whenever we grow cold, God uses these 'Ascension gift' people to remind us of our first love, and challenge us to reset our hearts to come back to Him.

HELPING ONE ANOTHER

The future Queen Esther, before she was married, underwent a year-long process of beauty preparation, helped by seven maids and supervised by a man called Hegai. He was there to watch over her, and to make her ready, through special food and beauty treatments (Es.2:8-12).

Like Esther, we are also in a process of preparation. This is not just a personal matter, it includes others helping us, as well. We need to be willing to receive their help. When we meet together with other believers we can encourage one another, as we see our wedding day drawing ever closer (Heb.10:25) There are many different ways in which we can help one another to stay on track with God's plan, and not get distracted.

Think about other believers who are helping you in the 'beauty preparation process'.

What are some of the ways in which we are helping one another? Write them below.

If you are in a group you might want to share your thoughts with one another.

1.

_____

_____

_____

_____

_____

_____

2.

_____

3.

4.

Jesus sets us an example in John, chapter thirteen.
Read John 13:2-17
What example is He calling us to?

_____

_____

_____

_____

_____

_____

A new command I give you, Love one another. As I have loved you, so you must love one another.' (John 13:34)

The New Testament letters are full of ways in which this command from Jesus to love one another can be lived out, as we relate with one another.
Here are four 'one anothers' to write down and consider, as we help each other to get ready for our wedding day.

Col 3:13

_____

_____

James 5:16

_____

_____

_____

Rom 15:7

_____

_____

1 Peter 5:5

_____

_____

_____

TREASURE IN JARS OF CLAY

Outwardly, we may look nothing like a glorious Bride! The raw materials don't look especially promising - the Bride does not come ready-made! However, Paul the apostle describes us as being like treasure in jars of clay, and the power at work in us being of God, and not our own!

'But we have this treasure in jars of clay to show that this all-surpassing power is from God and not from us' (2 Cor.4:7).

God wants to stir us up to go on a deeper journey with Him, and also to encourage others to do the same. The end result will be that we will all know Jesus more, and we will be like Him.

John says about the children of God, *'what we will be has not yet been made known. But we know that when He appears, we shall be like Him'* (1 Jn.3:2).

There is a process of surrendering that has to happen, as we allow the Potter to shape us, and work on us, until we shine with His glory! When the day comes, the church will be ready. Paul wrote that the Lord Jesus *'will transform our lowly bodies so that they will be like his glorious body'* (Phil.3:21). We have no need to panic – it will be alright on the Wedding day!.

Prayer

'Now to Him who is able to do immeasurably more than all we ask or imagine, according to His power that is at work within us, to Him be glory in the church and in Christ Jesus throughout all generations, for ever and ever! Amen'

(Eph.3:20-21)

REVIEW 4

Look back and review the different Sentness interactives in this fourth section on Deeper with Jesus. Write down one or two thoughts from each.

Deeper with Jesus – Interactive 16

_____

_____

_____

_____

_____

Beauty Preparations – Interactive 17

_____

_____

_____

_____

_____

YOUR NEXT STEP

There before me was a door standing open in Heaven... 'Come up here and I will show you what must take place after this' (Rev. 4:1)

Well done for going on a journey through this Sentness Interactive!

As you finish, what do you sense that God is saying to you about YOUR NEXT STEP forward?

Listen quietly, and then write down what your thoughts.

_____

_____

_____

_____

_____

_____

_____

_____

_____

_____

_____

_____

_____

LIST OF IMAGES

Perfume bottle
https://pxhere.com/en/photo/1212813
Arrow release   copyright free -source not known
Dandelion   copyright free -source not known
Keys
Bunch of keys from https://www.hippopx.com/sl/query?q=keys
Precious Jewels
https://www.publicdomainpictures.net/pictures/160000/velka/celtic-jewels.jpg
Painting Set
https://www.flickr.com/photos/didmyself/9390588145
Daniel Kulinski Flickr
Line of fishermen
https://www.flickr.com/photos/volvob12b/33426274976
Woven Basket
terryatkinson.typepad.com
Father with children   copyright free -source not known
Parenting Discovery Bubbles
Photo by form PxHere
Strawberry plants   copyright free -source not known
Village Community walk
copyright free -source not known
Writing a letter
Image by Free photos from Pixabay
At the feet of Jesus
copyright free -source not known
Mole hills
Image by **Ulrike Mai** from **Pixabay**
Presenting the Bride
Courtesy of Matt Dartford Photography
Wedding preparations
copyright free -source not known
Open Door
Image by Manfred Antranias Zimmer from Pixabay

'Sent' answers for page 51
Exodus 3 has five 'sents' in
vv10, 12, 13, 14 and 15,
and four 'go's in
vv10, 11, 16 and18.

'Rabbit Warren' communications from page 111
Our attempt at mapping the rabbit warren!

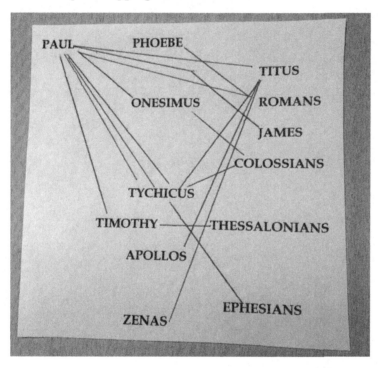

BOOKS FROM
OPEN WELLS PUBLISHING

BY THE SAME AUTHORS

Becoming Multi-flavoured Church
Singing over Havering
Prayer Walking around Redbridge
Launching after Lockdown
Sentness
Sentness Interactive

Poems by Mary Bain:
My Song Matters
Beyond the Door

*Available from **Amazon** or **www.lulu.com***

God on the Move
A fifty minute film –
Youtube search for
"God on the Move - Havering"
Welcome Network youtube channel

Other resources available on welcomenetwork.org

To God be the Glory!

Printed in Great Britain
by Amazon

40507010R00116